NICK WARE

THE BEAUTIFUL PLACE

GW00702020

FIERY HEDGE POETRY

THE BEAUTIFUL PLACE

First published 2018 by Fiery Hedge Publications

ISBN 978-0-9930473-6-7

Cover design and photography by Nick Ware assisted by Lewes Epps

Printed by CreateSpace

Nick Ware

THE BEAUTIFUL PLACE

Contents

To Chris, with whom I "slip the cordon", and those "striding away/up the nomad path" of the following generations – Kathryn, Matthew and David (the first), Timothy and Guinevere (the second)

And a child has also a picture of human existence peculiar to himself, which he probably never remembers after he has lost it: the original vision of the world. I think of this picture or vision as that of a state in which the earth, the houses on the earth, and the life of every human being are related to the sky overarching them; as if the sky fitted the earth and the earth the sky. Certain dreams convince me that a child has this vision, in which there is a completer harmony of all things with each other than he will ever know again.
EDWIN MUIR: AN AUTOBIOGRAPHY

Guess we're gonna have to learn to live again in this world.
RODDY FRAME: AUTUMN FLOWER

CHATELAINES

1. KATHERINE PARR

Four husbands in and Seymour's
all an ex-Queen could wish:
young, handsome, debonair;
the courtly stereotype –
yet not without ambition,
given the interest shown
in his nephew, the King
(and Katherine's stepson), Edward.

Meanwhile, the Dowager –
ever the pragmatist,
despite the infatuation
allowed by Henry's death –
presides over the Manor
with all the enterprise
of an experienced consort:
conspiring in the "horseplay"
between her rakish spouse
and young Elizabeth,
she comprehends the danger;
her ward's despatched elsewhere.

If Thomas manifests
affront and swears it meant
nothing, he joins his wife
at Winchcombe, nonetheless.
For her, the months ahead
will seem the culmination
of years when head ruled heart,
duty trumped preference –
this once – in an alliance
ventured for love, not fear;
joy, not material comfort.

The pregnancy will sweeten
their union even more.

And, although complications
around their daughter's birth
precipitate the end,
she meets it in the arms
that pleased her best – Lord Thomas
voicing astonishment
that she could die like this,
a woman in her prime
with happiness in view.

Sudeley Castle, 1548

2. EMMA DENT

Three centuries on and in
more comfortable times
than Katherine's, Emma Dent
numbers the miles she's walked
and the guests entertained
over the full twelve months
since the last reckoning.

Beside the annual
statistics, she records
her fondness for the planting
of the beech avenue,
imagines how the play
of shadows on the light
their leaves disperse will look
when none remember her.

The diary will protract
further the interim
in which her name's recalled:
spouse and companion
of the industrious John,
faithfully executing
during her widowed years
plans for the home they shared
and wider neighbourhood –
developments in keeping,
sympathetic repairs,
new trees, the covered walks,
mains water in the town.

Anecdotes intersperse
the progress of their schemes
with other narratives
describing foreign travel,
theatre, philanthropy,

beliefs and superstitions,
collected artefacts.

Various and informed,
the details humanise
this lonely matriarch –
one of those erudite
Victorian dignitaries
who understood aright
their station and their place.

Sudeley Castle, 1891

ON STRUMBLE HEAD

Fishguard then Goodwick and still time enough
for these mazy lanes – between high banks and trees –
scrambling onto the headland. Parked, we leave the car,
the cases and the maps, and tread the sward
above the sound – this sudden gust of sky
unhousing everything that's been curtailed
by needs-must, work-induced utility.

This morning, early, the escape: M5,
M4, the roads beyond, their distant views
of coast appearing – more than comfortably
in advance of the scheduled sailing – and this hour
with nothing wanted, all the Irish Sea
opening westward off the side of Wales.
Leisured, we note the purpling heather bells,
the lichen's yellow sunburst on the rocks
below the lighthouse, watch and memorise
the sequence of the lamp's revolving pulse
(*you'll* know its signal, entering these same waters
in darkness next weekend on the trip home.)

Back at the car, we sit, read, feel the sense
of urgency that's goaded all year long
disperse like thistledown upon the currents
that govern in this vaster atmosphere
of wind and tide: that other world's no more
than distant rumour – so much so, we'd stay,
except the ferry bound for port recalls
the day's itinerary. We stow the books
and, trundling down the lanes beneath the cape,
approach the dock with customary haste.

FOREPLAY

No less than the moments
of mutual ecstasy,
each stage of intimacy
that conducts us there.

TRANSITIONS

East in the morning: clouds and sun
overhead in equal measure up
the motorway – your adept grip
on the steering (right foot pedal down)

round slower traffic, mind intent
on Norfolk's restless shore, the tide
chafing its cliffs. I'm at your side,
similarly impatient

with distance: landscapes hurtle by,
affording glimpses of the past
– Wiltshire, its chalk escarpments massed
against the early-summer sky,

where Kathryn slid into the light
for the first time that afternoon
and changed with her incursion
everything since. It was last night

we heard the news – "Timothy Jack,
4.27, five pounds twelve…"
(*"Kat weighed no more at birth herself!"*)
Now, this interminable trek,

this pushing on into the day
that holds the rich potential
of that first grandchild – waiting, small
and almost England's width away.

*

I was also the passenger
on the evening we hastened west
down the A30 and over
its two moors, winter's last frost

glistening along the carriageway
beneath headlamps. We'd had the call
before and, immediately,
entered the slide, that near-freefall

descent we'd anticipated
with Dad's inexorable decline
in those last weeks (hospital bed,
the dull purr of piped oxygen.)

And, so, the heaving dark, with hours
remaining: still, we held the road
– from Bodmin, all curves and contours –
until Wadebridge and the subdued

apartment, voices lowered round
his hopelessly beleaguered frame.
No doubting, there, how near the end
or wishing it was not his time.

In the next morning's grey, we missed
the passing – typically discreet –
though much it quietly erased
informs the living moment yet.

UNDELIVERABLE

Tim, it's some time since I updated you
on things round here. How is the life beyond?
And would you choose it over these mixed climes,
if all were in your scope? Well, anyway,
they still afford some reason for deferring
the journey hence. Work's an anxiety,
it's true, devouring evenings and weekends
peremptorily – the spectre at the feast.
There's solace, even so, in other things,
the ordinary yet miraculous:
sunlight and birdsong – these, invariably,
will elevate – though, often, I'll admit,
I've sunk my troubling thoughts in ale or wine.

Not that it helps: what lifts me more is how
the children are, granted allowable
with me that juvenile designation when
one's married, one's at uni and the third
seeking employment – adults, all of them,
and variously establishing themselves
in an adult world. Somehow, the characters
we watched emerging in their childhood years
persist, though none's readily pigeon-holed –
fully themselves, the personality
of each unique, albeit each displays
parental traits and others that maintain
an ancestry that reaches further back
and severally appears upon the stem
of the family tree. In Matthew's impish humour,
I've glimpsed something of Grandad and of you.
David resembles Dad: *his* death, last year,
puts him in your domain, if the truths claimed
deliver. Funny that – like him, the third
and youngest – David bears his image strongly:
speaking and standing in his routine pose,

Dad's there. And yet it's David, nonetheless –
despite inheritance, original.

And, at this juncture, here's the latest: Kat's
a mother, now – the baby has your name.
Holding him yesterday in the hospital,
we saw the mild, uncomprehending eyes
of the new-born open momentarily
then close as if the life that greeted them
might overwhelm – so much of it, at once,
and so soon (though I'll hazard this life's more
than any will admit unchecked or straight,
its vastness, wildness and intensity
searing the mind with white-hot violence.)

Whatever he becomes, he'll be himself –
boy and man – never mind the heritage
implied, the loaded name. Holding him, though,
I thought of you and what, with you, we lost;
how you, like him, were held during those days
five decades back. Nobody, then, imagined
we'd mourn you nearly half that interval;
and yet, although you've no direct descent,
I've kept you with me all these silent years
(you or the ghost of you my memories shape.)
You'll never wholly die while I exist
or, when I'm dead, while others still recall
something of you or I. And, once they've passed,
neither will matter much: what's handed down
will manifest itself with scant regard
for history, ignorant of the lives before.

The elder, I defended you at school:
you grew and stood secure among your peers
without my questionable patronage;
travelled – alone, with others – saw the peak
of Everest at sunrise and the glow
of afternoon suffuse the Taj Mahal

with honeyed warmth. And, though it's so much more
than most will see who live their full threescore
and ten, it grieves – the sense of what you missed,
my impotence to stay the bully's hand.

11th May, 2014

VIKING RAID RE-ENACTMENT, LINDISFARNE

The Danes have landed: mobile
aloft, one warrior
holds back, reporting home
with word of their safe arrival.

HOLY ISLAND

How we imagine it is separate,
reflected light dappling the lifted wave –
another world, almost, tide-bound and solitary.

So – once its intervening wash subsides –
the truth affronts: vehicles in convoy
winding inland; the overrun green field

prepared for their coming; day visitors
(among them, us) converging on the village
in search of coffee and conveniences.

After these comforts, the hordes disperse:
between the castle and the priory,
diminished columns waver and straggle –

caught in the open, strafed with off-shore winds,
disarmed by nature's vigorous onslaught
and strewn about the meadows and the sands.

We sense around us the preserve of saints!
Retreating by the causeway at the end
of the afternoon, it is with distance

we comprehend its isolation –
how depths renewed secure the probity
of the beautiful loneliness we didn't find.

THE LIGHT WELL

Inside the curtain wall,
scenes of collapse: the grid
of stone meshed in the grass;
heraldic posturings
over the ruptured pile.

The keep (somewhat apart
and virtually intact)
afforded us more sense
of the interior world
it quartered in its time:
cellar and scullery,
kitchen and banqueting hall,
the earl's sequestered rooms.

Between these fixed domains,
the open vertical
diffusing light, the vent
admitting truer air
than otherwise might sweeten
a wasps' nest of ambition,
intrigue and appetite.

The light well, it was called:
via its sump, the day
inundated the stronghold,
appraising on its tide
the pattern of events –
momentous and mundane
alike – the laudable,
the ignominious.

Coming at it among
those purblind passages,
we saw immediately

its startling influence:
how the sun's rays perused
the murky labyrinth,
revealed the bastion's heart.

It's often struck me, since –
that notion of a shaft
within, light filtering down
into the recesses
below, the vague abode
of motive and intent.

The thought attracts me, still,
and I'll confess the need
of – somewhere in myself –
an aperture of grace
that permeates the dark,
informs the depths beneath.

Warkworth, Northumberland

GRACE DARLING

Her life was one of those
defined by a single act:
utterly obscure,
until the Farnes
despatched the *Forfarshire*.

The 7th of September,
1838:
monumental tides –
her literal watershed.

*

Grace Horsley Darling.

The name was apt enough
in the minds of those
she observed – with morning,
visible on the rock.

For hours, they'd clung on
in the heaving dark:
first light revealed
their predicament fully.

*

Grace – meaning kindness
or mercy, even, shown
irrespective of merit
and with no regard
for entitlement.

Darling – term
of endearment. Ever
and always the family's;
henceforward, the nation's.

*

But that future fame
never occurred
as she strained at the oars
(paired with her father),

directing the coble
into the strait,
across treacherous seas –

with no thought in her peril
but possible rescue.

*

Two hours in the boat
and, all around, the storm.

Two days in the lighthouse, likewise –
the saved and their saviours
subsisting in those cramped quarters –
until the storm abated.

Then, afterwards, the storm
of publicity: one that raged
for her remaining lifetime.

*

Named by the press,
her name became the lure
that hauled in artist, tourist
(visitor on visitor,
expected or otherwise);

and the gifts, the letters,
the adulation –
wave after wave,
converging on the Longstone.

*

None of this sought
and much an unwelcome
intrusion on the life
known since infancy:

duties performed for themselves
and the needs they served –
watches maintained,
nets mended,
lanterns kept.

*

Ill at ease
with celebrity
and, then, just ill,

she slipped the grasp
of theatre, circus,
even the church
(their claimed endorsements),

in answering the one claim
that's universal.

*

Most miss the simple grave
for the ornate
Victorian memorial –

as, in the deed, they missed
the shyly steadfast character
of the Bamburgh child

who, at all times
and in all circumstances,
did what she must.

Bamburgh, Northumberland

BENEATH THE ANGEL OF THE NORTH

Round here,
they could do with some angels,
though the one they've got
aligns itself
with gods of coal and steel –

gods who've abandoned
this populace
for the furnaces
that smoulder in the East.

The industry's set sail:
its ministrants
languish beside
the old machinery
that let them down.

In the Metro Centre,
on the banks that hold the Tyne,
new deities
establish their command.

But this angel stands
apart
on its hillside,
like the rescuer
deployed in times of siege

who comes too late
to intervene or save
and stops short,
knowing the venture's futile.

*

Whom does it serve,
this stanchion, this
soaring colossus?

Wings hefted, held,
positioned on the spine,
shouldered,

steady
and unwavering
in the afternoon –

whom does it serve?
Redundant labourers?
Men who defined themselves

by how they earned
and sign on, now,
with conscious unease?

If these at all,
only the memory:
shipyards and steelworks shut,

collieries de-commissioned –
their poverty
the human detritus

in the market's shift,
their meagre lives
worthless collateral.

*

Or pioneers
of the information age?

They're more intent
upon aerials other

than the one mounted
against *this* sky.

The airwaves seethe
with local noise,

beguile the ear
with distant rumours:

siren songs,
competing messages

in the traffic roar –
the tide of unrest

that contains the silence met
at its vast transmitter.

*

Or maybe tourists,
much like you and I,
who – pulling off
the southbound carriageway
of the A1
on this August weekday –

make the diversion
that ends up
under this mast,
the mute totem
this dying culture set
over its demise?

*

Face, expressionless;
stance, remote –

the figure, not
of this dimension

(if solid enough
amid urban skies),

its stillness
alien

in the vast maze
encircling the space

where it stands its ground.
For everyone.

Or no one.

*

Yet, whatever else informed
the commissioning
of this local titan,

its angled wings
communicate
the notion of embrace

and infer the substance
of what's needed most:
some angel of the roads

that meets us –
anxious, circling, miles off course –
enfolds us with compassion

and sets us straight;
that oversees
and keeps our wandering souls

(even though they stray)
along the homeward path.

ON A VOCATIONAL HEAD

He felt the urgent
call of the priesthood
– the sooner the biretta.

*

That guy in the big hat
was a bishop.

Mitre known.

LATE RISER

Noon breakfast – toast cold
and, over soggy cornflakes,
the day's new milk warm.

TIME PIECE

with apologies to Andrew Sparke, who wrote something similar

The two most uncomfortable moments in your day:
ache o' clock in the morning and ache o' clock at night.

FROM THE POETRY BUREAU

Humorous poetry:
where wit displays its talents.

*

Romantic poetry:
where love declares its hand.

*

Nostalgic poetry:
where memories are archived.

*

The poetry of grief:
where you put the pain.

AUTUMN MORNING, LINCOLN

On the east side of the country,
we part the curtains as the earth's
face reappears. Last night, we saw
the Devon hills receding, felt
the dark world pass beneath. The stars
were muffled in the orange glow
of neon, but – now – the nearest
reddens the ridge that meets the eye
at this hotel window, spilling
over the cityscape between:
trees, high-rise buildings, retail park.

THE BEAUTIFUL PLACE

Not on any map that I know of, it exists
somewhere and everywhere, seen or unseen,
elusive and indistinct: dreams hedge the path there
and unravel their maze capriciously.
So – once or twice in an entire decade –
waking, I'll half-remember being there
in sunlight among the lakeside trees,
caressed by the moist wind, or walking uphill
towards the summit and its heady view
of all that rolls beneath, the vast canvas
stretching away in yellows, greens and blues.

Almost immediately, the vision fades:
the details lose their sharpness and I'll know,
thereafter, only the pain of exile –
sweet in itself, although the intensity
diminishes by the day, week, month and year –
until the next time sleep abandons me
shy of the mark. Meanwhile, the ordinary world
imposes with its cares and its demands –
work or the thousand mundane tyrannies
that rule the home – though, underneath them, still,
the thought persists of spheres that lie beyond
their impatient jurisdiction.

                              Into these realms,
the unconscious mind will inadvertently
stumble at times and – on the edge of sight –
glimpse something other momentarily:
enough that in my memory it sustains
the memory of the memory of the scene
while morning after morning overwrites
what drew the eye with harsh imperatives.

What stays with me's the notion of the sense

of unity – of oneness with all things –
encountered there, so much at variance with
and otherwise than how things are or seem
in the everyday: the same impressions
inform the landscapes dreamed in adulthood
that once suffused the glance of infancy.
And, while what's apprehended in this state
of sleep may integrate that distant past
with intimations of another world,
it's in the current and imperfect *here* –
the *now* we share – that, intermittently,
if mind and circumstances correlate,
we slip the cordon of anxiety
and venture upon the beautiful, awake.

THE MAWDDACH TRAIL: DOLGELLAU TO BARMOUTH

1. CAE MARIAN

Start where you are:
on the meadow, looking back
at the slate and stone
of the snug-shouldered town
hemmed in under the mountain.

Ahead, Afon Wnion
and – where you'll pass,
winding among birches
along its spate –
walkers ebbing west.

You observe the trend,
follow the path downstream,
find the far bank
via the metal span
and – in moments, almost –

the meadow shrugs you off,
that first panorama
removing by degrees
without ever disclosing
its vanishing point.

2. BEYOND PONT-Y-WERNDDU

Poised by a shoal
of glistening gravel,

head down,
the dipper nods you on

up the disused track-bed:
the aisle implied

(avoiding the river junction)
leads by default between

these over-arching trees.
Out under the skies,

stealing among the reeds,
the Mawddach glides

steadily closer,
while you march this lane where –

at any second – winds
might charge you down. Like trains.

3. PENMAENPOOL

Oddly, the first
eponymous encounter
yields more lagoon
than tidal stream –
the headland-harboured,
near-backwater
favouring the settlement
with a Wenglish name.

Milling into view
as the trail opens
on the straight run
past the old Great Western signal,
it warrants pause –
this landscape hymned by Hopkins,
with whom concur
those stopped at the hotel.

4. ON THE ESTUARY

Its shelf
thrust between two
opposing mountain chains,

circuitously,
the river
negotiates

the swirling channels
of its creek
and sandbank maze.

*

And the shelf widens,
its watery sill

mirroring ever more sky
with its seaward sortie;

while, on either side,
the hills

fall back
respectfully.

5. AT MORFA MAWDDACH

Left, now, with one
platform working of the five
that served their prime,
the last rails sweep around

and meet the trail
for the final leg,
their ballast deep
in marram grass and sand.

Cyclists dismount, ramblers
locate their maps and themselves
at the tables placed
for their refurbishment.

Needful hiatus,
it's what it's always been:
neither here nor there –
merely the lapse between.

6. VIEW FROM THE BRIDGE, BARMOUTH

What lies behind –
not what's ahead.

The journey –
not the destination.

The glacial valley
leading the eye, again,

between ranges, back
among origins –

not the Irish Sea,
a murmur in the haze

beyond the sandspit,
quietly kept at bay.

The buoyant river
launching reflected suns

off its upturned wave,
one glittering firmament –

not the tourist town,
touting its heritage

in the erstwhile chapel
bargain antique stores.

What lies behind –
not what's ahead.

The journey –
not the destination.

7. RETURN

by bus,
rumbling down
the other side
of the estuary –

distant
window seat glimpses
of the landscapes
where you hit your stride.

GRANDCHILD WAKING

Up in the dark – the thought of work already
imposing on my morning consciousness –
I hear the mobile start in the back bedroom
and know sleep's at an end with him, like me.

Over and over, the tinkling strain
repeats – slow and unhurried – while I time
alarm calls, cups of tea, stagger events
around the onset of the coming day.

Behind the door, he tries his voice: I catch
its intermittent murmur on the stair –
that mild experiment with sound and sense,
the coo of conversation with himself.

How it delights! No trouble or concern
diminishes his waking happiness:
he greets the dawn, content – aware of nothing
beside the tranquil moment in his grasp.

CONSTITUTIONAL

Mid-winter, mid-afternoon: slipping
the home's inertia, you stroll
about the estate that's twined itself
across this shoulder of the hill –

gardens asleep, their life withdrawn
into the stillness that contains
the muted landscape, bedded down
for the season. As early dusk

curtails vision, in darkening rooms,
lamps wink on, start sporadically
amid the near opacity
of the houses they illuminate.

Attracted by these sparks of warmth
and colour in the general fade,
the eyes stray momentarily
over the scenes the light's displayed:

companionable indolence
around the television
or, at the table, amusements
with games or other pastimes. How

relaxed – fully themselves – how true
those figures look! Watching, you might
imagine them content – as they
might, gazing out, imagine you.

MAY

and the rain
drives in off the coast,

greening
the new leaves,
the abundant grass;

fingers drumming
their light tattoo –
mild

and incessant –
on tile, on window;
permeating

the mind within;
quickening memory
and emotion;

making vivid
its sounds
and images

with all the soaked
intensity

of grief.

IN THE PICTURE

for Guinevere Saoirse

I have glimpsed that heartland –
the green slant of its hills –
in the grain of your mother's
early crayoning:
there, children dance, joyful,
their upturned mouths
wide with delight,
like brimming chalices.

With luck, you'll inherit
her propensity
for laughter, mirth,
the articulation –
in wax or chalk
or other medium –
of that overflow,
that unchecked infant cheer.

And, if – in time –
the troubles that attend
your growing years
inhibit or stifle
the gladness within,
imposing sorrow's scrawl
on the favoured landscape,
may you still recall

how it was at the first:
find joy in the moment
and keep always alive
in your inmost self
the dancing child
and the smile that says,

in this sad old world,
there's no happier place.

OLYMPUS

Swift as the lightning, Zeus found true renown
habitually by putting women down.

Hera, his wife, assumed the jealous part,
perceiving not the victim but the tart.

Athena, wise enough yet petulant,
was similarly given to affront.

Mortal Cassandra scorned Apollo's bed,
and saw the path of misery ahead.

Though Aphrodite's beauty had the sway
of Paris, Troy burned for her vanity!

Lame Hephaestos, with due diligence,
perfected the supply of armaments.

If other members of the pantheon
held back, the curses of their peers worked on.

Under the living world, enthroned in Hell,
Hades did nothing, watched his remit swell.

War at an end, Odysseus was no better:
he faced Poseidon's decade-long vendetta.

And, still, it soars – that legendary height –
inspiring virtue, excellence and might.

Or so it would appear, unless you quarrel
with any stance that holds immortals moral.

And, centuries on, we contemplate the damage
that comes of making gods in one's own image.

THE SYRIAN QUESTIONS

What makes them go,
abandoning their homes,
their belongings – all
they've possessed or known –
staking everything
on the slender chance
of an unfit vessel
listing miles off the shore?

What makes them stay,
clambering among the ruins,
foraging for their needs
between the shells
that decimate
the human infrastructure –
dwelling, clinic,
sinew, skeleton?

What makes them choose
one or the other,
when neither option
offers the guarantee
of eventual safety?
What makes them decide
with hell behind
and, ahead, the indifferent sea?

Aleppo, 2016

IN SCARBOROUGH

1. ANNE BRONTE

Again, Wood's Lodgings: not the governess
(exploited, disregarded, patronised);
rather, this time, the accompanied guest.
Charlotte, sisterly, chafes at the madness
of the venture; Ellen, milder, keeps the peace.
Both love the invalid – if ill-advised
in their itinerary, still, they make the best,
despite the virulence of the disease.

Her hope's in heaven; first, though, one more look.
Beneath her window, lies the favoured bay –
above the shore, the old church with its clock.
On this spring afternoon, it's heavenly!
The end will happen nearly by the book:
death's Edward Weston; she – is Agnes Grey.

South Cliff, 1849

2. WILFRED OWEN

Efficiency's the order of the day
in the Clarence Gardens Hotel: its young lieutenant
marshals the household troops – buglers are sent
scurrying, chars upbraided waspishly.
During his leisure, domesticity
persists – round stores, at auctions – in the hunt
for pieces that fit the home imagined
once this attrition's shrapnel-memory.

Strolling up Queen's Parade, he hears the boom
below as waves assail the undercliff;
the cries of *soldiers* reach him in his room.
He's witnessed hell; now, the imperative
detonates in him poem on poem
that ordinary pursuits will not relieve.

North Bay, 1917

WHERE

Where you overlap with me in time and space;
where our minds and bodies coincide intimately.

Where – somewhere – sunlight alters the perceptions;
where it illuminates the landscape's manuscript.

Where employment satisfies intrinsically;
where it affords time, besides, for life.

Where happiness bests anxiety;
where nothing diminishes the moment's elation.

Where strangers are met with kindness;
where it informs attitudes more than suspicion.

AT WESTONBIRT ARBORETUM

October morning:
mist low, but the flames rise – deep
in the Acer Grove.

Gloucestershire

SUPPORTER

Saturdays, we
head for the game:
Up the City –
that's their name

(*Town*, *Athletic*
or *United*,
seeking to make
their title bid!)

Tickets, turnstiles,
tiered stands;
chants and yells,
discordant bands.

For ninety minutes,
end to end,
forty-four boots
challenge, defend,

pass the ball, run,
distract, create
and – with good fortune –
find the net.

We cheer the team,
berate the ref;
dispute the claim,
applaud the save;

endure the stalemate,
mourn the loss;
jubilate,
if victorious.

If, years ahead,
you're at the Park –
you and *your* kid
or kids (the spark

of interest kindled
long before
routinely fuelled
by the next fixture) –

remember how
we'd shoehorn in,
elbow to elbow,
for the home win

and, in the crush,
would share the joy
(likewise, the anguish),
man and boy.

RETIREMENT PROSPECT

One of these days, if you've not died in harness first,
the shift will end and there'll be no more shifts.
Or none you'll work. Instead, you'll clear your desk,
empty your locker, walk away with all
you've kept intact of what you started with
or what you made of it during your years
of answering the claims of the machine.

And, chances are (assuming you've maintained
some kind of ethic), there'll be accolades:
the public valediction, the gift
engraved with universal well wishes,
pages of individual messages
expressive of your qualities with peers
who'll miss those given merits when withdrawn.

Acquaintance by these means with what you've meant
will weigh on you – oppress more than relieve –
since, in absconding, you'll negate that much
thereafter in the setting that afforded
your eminence: their loss will seem your own
and what you are unbodied where, if ever
you pass, you'll enter only as a ghost.

You've left your post before, have borne the ache
of separation, engaged elsewhere
(with some adjustment), but – this time – the sense
of permanence will creep unnervingly
around your soul, chill and infect it with
an irrevocable and greater glimpse
of what's inferred in all those little deaths.

HYMN TO LIFE

We praise the origin – the source
of all we are – that lives, that moves,
within us on whatever course
survival urges or approves;

that forms the organs, knits the bones
and animates the mouth, the eyes;
suffuses arteries and veins;
informs the vigour of the thighs

and swells their locus with desire
which will, aroused, so inundate
the body's field no reason for
desisting will prevent the spate.

We praise, though – once its impetus
diverts into another stream –
onward momentum slows in us,
the currents stall with nature's whim;

praise, though the confluence dissipates
in mud and silt, while life moves on;
praise, though the life that navigates
these conduits will desert each one,

contriving by this artifice
transcendence of the shoals ahead.
Its agents, still, the life we praise –
the living, by that life betrayed.

DECEMBER

The gold of the leaves has tarnished,
the light that brought them currency withdrawn:
discarded, now, they spill along the path –
their brilliance fading, like the afternoon –
until the mounds lie, brown and uniform,
over the blurring landscape.

                        Wistfully,
I stray among them, cherishing within
images of their brief autumnal blaze:
the memories that I'll wear across the heart
during winter's chill – the bright against the blue.

THE PRACTICE OF THE ABSENCE OF GOD

Indoors, there's enough
that occupies the mind
without its indulging
in metaphysics:
encroaching dust,
clutter, bacteria,
arresting which
engages thought and will,
diverts energies;
while, always – between bouts –
the media's clamour
insinuates,
secures the vacuum.

*

Outdoors, there's less
that holds in abeyance
what's unseen
and intangible
yet manifest
in the overtures
of ever-altering skies,
of timeless hills;
that keeps in check
the impulse these elicit –
its gathered sense
of thanks and amazement
that anything is.

AGNOSTIC

Less than certain and something more than in doubt,
you live the contradiction: surmise
the natural world's utter indifference,
divine no meaning in the glittering skies;
and yet concede at once the inference
of grace in the miracle of winter sunlight.

Or summer rain. However it's construed,
weather performs these benedictions.
Need won't deploy them or entitlement:
granted, withheld – it happens when it happens.
The common expectation: you count
on nothing, meet what comes with gratitude.

SPRING MURMUR

Trees –
bare all winter –
are yellowing up;

the fuzzed ends of twigs
on the small magnolia
scarcely contain
the gifts they hoard.

We're on the cusp,
the balance poised between
the long months of cold behind
and the heat foretold
by the softening wind.

It's that moment
of arrest
before the coming season
effects its cure

and the scales
tip back
towards summer.

IN THE MALVERNS

On these hills,
I mean nothing

or am at most
only the faintest

erosion
of the ground –

the import of my tread
no more

on the scales
than the thousands of others

traversing miles
of vertebrae.

*

Westward, swifts
mobbing the pair

of kestrels suspended
over green sward –

migrants troubling
the local regimen,

their lithe wings
unsettling the thermals.

*

Higher than these, even –
up

among the spurs
on the dinosaur's back

(jagged, incised) –
we look down, remark

how the human landscape's
miniaturised

in the vales
beneath:

their scatter
of settlements

on the living map
of small concern;

a matter
of perspective.

*

We descend
past benches

named for the dead
"who loved these hills" –

recalled
less for their deeds

than the ground
that sustained them.

*

For decades –
heading north –

we'd watched
and seen them loom,

mirage-like,
west of the motorway;

never, though,
before

approached
or stood

on their distant heights,
inviolable

in the haze.
Heights that, once scaled,

affirmed
my insignificance.

WRITE-OFF: POET VERSUS GRAFFITI ARTIST

On paper – not the uprights of the pier
or shadowed underpass (spelt or mis-spelt) –
what might I claim more true than "I was here"
but the addendum, "This is how life felt"?

GENERATIONS

Those lodged within me,
nestling beneath the skin
or surfacing in
gesture, expression, stance:

those still alive
and the recent dead
who overlapped with me
or coincide;

and those long deceased,
the ones who've slipped
the communal mind,
anonymised by time.

*

Those striding away
up the nomad path
whose lives will shelter
what persists of me:

those among whom
I share that DNA
which, when I'm dust,
will hold its memory;

and those unborn
who'll manifest its traits –
the populace where
I must lose myself.

HAPPISBURGH

Living here, you must abandon
the notion of permanence.
What matter the leaning fence?
The *house* will eventually fall.

Back (after an absence
of years) and the memory's
adrift, what's no longer there
skewing its sense of what is –

how the roads lie, how the cliffs
stand or surrender ground,
at odds with imagination.
Only the strenuous waves

persist, familiar enough:
these and – among crops – the lighthouse,
keeping well clear, aloof
of the shipwrecked shoreline's struggle.

August, 2017

BARMOUTH REVISITED

Honeymoon purchases,
the two ceramic mugs
acquired that first day in
at Woolworths saw the bin
long back: the business has,
like them, gone to the dogs.

If you've kept the bikini,
darling, you wouldn't wear
an item so revealing,
now (but the thought's appealing:
you in something skimpy!)
The boutique isn't there

any more. Life's moved on:
there are still cups of tea
and moments of undress;
also, we harbour – yes –
one genuine Welsh love spoon,
one Carole King LP.

September, 2017

DURING THE TORRENT WALK

Its woods
still wet
and slippery
with last year's leaf mould,
last night's rain,
the gorge
closes sky out
and us in.

Descending
warily
into the cleft,
our senses
are immersed
in sound and spume:

an overwhelming
and incessant
shooting arcade
within which
nature
wrestles nature down –

rock-fall,
tree-fall;
vivid moss
and creeper
spreading
implacably; all
this beautiful
devastation.

PERSPECTIVE

Believing faith equal
to doubt, I climbed the fence,
peered over and observed
that the other garden
was no less beautiful,
no more wild or unkempt,
than the one I had left.

Troubled, I clung on, weighed
up the alternatives
my view afforded – its
two landscapes much the same,
allowing even for
the differences in
interpretation.

Unable to decide
between them, it appeared
better that I take down
the barrier, admit
one garden within which
what matters isn't where
you stand – it's how you live.

WINTER IN THE HOUSE

1. MORNING

How you wake and know, at once, that there's been frost.

How the boiler coughs into huffish industry.

How the bed curbs other imperatives.

How the sun warms with colour ceiling, walls.

How the day warrants a second cup of tea.

2. AFTERNOON

How the scents of Christmas mingle in the bowl.

How the light's wash erupts with liquid flame.

How the stew thickens gently on the stove.

How, imperceptibly, dusk closes in.

How wine inures against the lengthening dark.

HEREAFTERWARDS

What seasons will we know
in the life beyond this one?
With no death, no decay,
what process will allow
or stage transition?
Unless others make way,

how will new things become?
How will nature preserve
their everlasting verve?
And with what mechanism
stay the ephemeral
complexions of the fall?

FOR THE JOURNEY

Jesus did many other things as well. If every one of them
were written down, I suppose that even the whole world
would not have room for the books that would be written.
JOHN 21: 25

So, after two millennia, there's still
space on the shelves, still room for even more,
albeit much they hold's not of the Saviour
or what he taught, despite its substantial

impact on the literary body
this planet quarters (meaning no offence,
evangelist, for the said inference;
just that the boast remains hyperbole.)

Books, though, are on the increase, all the same,
in ever-varying formats: physical
or – in this modern era – virtual,
which somewhat alleviates the problem

of storage. They come in every genre
imaginable and some you'd not believe –
profound or witty, erudite or naïve,
their content mundane or spectacular.

One might question, given their prevalence,
the merit of this constant writing down:
what's vindicated in composition
and – if any at all – the difference

it makes; if it instructs or entertains,
conserves the memories or affords the soul
some kind of stake in the material,
even when dead. Whichever, it sustains

the theme or narrative for longer than
voice alone will. Over the centuries, books
have burned for their opinions – in the mix,
the sacred or subversive or profane.

This notwithstanding, many still survive
that at one time or other were supressed,
inspiring in humanity the best
and worst interpretations of the archive:

its salvaged truths, its harboured fictions,
treatises on experience, debate
between all sides on ethics or the state,
continually exert their influence

upon the species, in whatever code;
and will, maybe, until the species ends –
its works abrading on the planet's winds
with all that long-held wisdom of the road.

DEPARTURES

1. THE SWALLOWS

I heard them mustering along the lane
that ran behind the College and my view
over the fields that morning, all that day,
was scythed with wings – adept, impatient
to vault the near horizon, leave the sky
around as vacant as the land below.

Before a week had passed, they'd disappeared.
I sensed it in the muteness of the air:
at once expectant and bereft, the thermals
missing the sweep, the tilt, the sinuous turn;
awaiting something other.

                        Year upon year,
since then, I've known it: suddenly, that heightened
perception of the transience of things –
of standing grain, the scent of summer grass,
the swallows' restless patterns overhead.
So quickly past! Now, this sad radiance
suffuses everything they've left behind
and will itself diminish, like the days
this side of the solstice, waning into dusk
with all the gravitas of grace withdrawn.

Once, I'd imagine winging home, like them,
migrating to some region beyond
the earth's sparse cage, where light's hemmed in – where
                                   shadows
traverse its wintry marches, imposing
their shapes with menace on the tranquil glow
of afternoon. These days, I'm of the mind
that home is where I am – with any weather
or circumstance the context will allow –

and, being here, that life's the lovelier for
the full twelve months of variation
between the alternating warmth and cold.

I'd keep the cycle, cherish every shift
and change encountered on that beautiful
and wandering circuit more than an envisaged
state of eternal summer (arguably,
mere stasis, I'd suggest); and yet, perhaps –
with my last winter on me and the future
entirely dark, hope dead, the night wind chill –
were passage offered, I might emulate
those migrants glimpsed on wires above the house
whose hubbub has dispersed with moving on.

2. THE LEAVES

Spiralling off trees and calendars
along the track of the declining year –
its campaign veterans – the leaves break rank,
soar upon wintry squalls whose violations
litter with dead culvert and avenue.

And, so, I watch summer evacuate
the landscape – hillside, hedgerow, this exposed
garden, half-wilderness yet – observe the light
kindling upon the branches and the brief
candescence of the flares those last leaves raise,
their frail ribs pierced with an intensity
that meets an answering signal in the heart.
The impulse, always – sweet, ambivalent
with longing – mounts within me, gathering
onward momentum, as successive autumns
sweep me into their decimated lanes.

However rich their late luxuriance,
there's something that's unhealed – awry – in me
that needs this annual conflagration,
these sparks erupting on the restless breeze
and spinning in its wake, until their flames
gutter among the spillage on the path;
that holds this last display in more esteem,
almost, than any other; that perceives
the import of its shared trajectories
above the stark, inevitable earth.

Of all that flesh embodies – everything
contained within its husk – what will survive
its downfall? What will mitigate its end?

My questions weigh with nightfall: walking home,
I scuff the leaf mould, stir and unsettle
its trail of spent illuminations

(colourless in the murk, life's flicker gone);
and, still, these eyes interrogate the dusk
that hides the vivid world – in trust, in doubt,
negotiate the intervening miles
of winter dark, lights waiting in the house.

Notes on The Beautiful Place

Virtually all the poems that make up this collection were completed after April 2013, though some were conceived earlier – several of them by decades. However, the thinking that informs its content is unquestionably current. Despite the appearance between them of *Subdued Anthems* and *Strange Country*, *The Beautiful Place* provides the genuine successor to *Perception of Light*, these other volumes being comprised mainly of much older material.

On Strumble Head references the summer of 2013 and was originally the preferred opener. If it deserved that status, only my sense of chronology demanded that *Chatelaines* went in ahead, given the overlap it affords with *Gloucestershire Spring* and the "stately ruins" described in that penultimate poem of *Perception of Light*. The historical pairing of Katherine Parr with Emma Dent was an obvious one after visiting the exhibitions about these individuals at Sudeley Castle.

Irrespective of the time lapse between them, *Undeliverable* continues the somewhat one-sided correspondence inaugurated with *Millennium Letter* in *Dismantling No Man's Land* (*Subdued Anthems.*)

Grace Darling came to my attention when visiting Northumberland during 2014. Her heroism intrigued me enough to research her life further, largely via the Internet. The sequence that follows hers in the collection, *Beneath the Angel of the North*, was similarly conceived and informed.

There's little more to *On a Vocational Head* than two bad puns (three if you include its title.) The idea of this small and admittedly quite silly sequence originated with Seamus Heaney's poem, *The Biretta* (*Seeing Things*.)

Aches in Andrew Sparke's collection *Broken English* should explain the apology at the start of *Time Piece*. Hopefully, it's sufficient recompense for this minor literary theft.

Graham and Jacky O'Hanlon's *Explore the Mawddach Trail* informed and supplemented walks along the route during the composition of *The Mawddach Trail: Dolgellau to Barmouth*. The sequence may not do justice to the landscape that it traverses but captures, even so, some elements of the experience. The rather disparaging reference to the "tourist town" at the end of it is, arguably, somewhat unfair. I suspect that it would need more than *Barmouth Revisited* to redress the balance fully. However, there's always the next volume of poetry...

The referenced holiday resort suggested the pair of sonnets that constitute *In Scarborough*. Anne Bronte's grave and the display in St Mary's Church inspired the first, the blue plaque on the Clifton Hotel the second. Other sources included Juliet Barker's *The Brontes* and Jon Stallworthy's *Wilfred Owen*.

Elements of an older poem were incorporated more successfully into *In the Picture*. The original was something of an admonition to my eldest child, Kathryn, upon entering formal education; the final version transfers its attention to *her* daughter, but the sentiments are much the same.

I'm indebted to *Every* in Wendy Cope's *Anecdotal Evidence* for the overall structure of *Where*, whether or not the connection's apparent.

Brother Lawrence's *The Practice of the Presence of God* encouraged the idea of an oppositely titled poem, one that explored the challenges of the alternative imagined.

An experience at Westminster College, Oxford, in September 1983, gave me the basis for *The Swallows*. Older and considerably differing versions of this and of *The Leaves* were, at one time, intended to appear in *The Songs of Exile* (*Subdued Anthems*), but they never really satisfied me and were, in the event, excluded. In consequence, the two *Departures* poems that finish this collection are as I'd wish at this stage in my life.

Thanks, as ever, go to Chris, my wife, who's lived – more supportively than it sometimes merits – with my musing nature. More widely, I'm thankful to everyone else kind enough to show interest in the material that's resulted.

Fiery Hedge Publications

Fiery Hedge Information:

https://www.facebook.com/fieryhedgepoetry

www.fieryhedge.wordpress.com

Also by Nick Ware:

Perception of Light **(November, 2014)**

Subdued Anthems: Back Catalogue, Volume 1 **(September, 2015)**

Strange Country: Back Catalogue, Volume 2 **(November, 2015)**

Printed in Great Britain
by Amazon